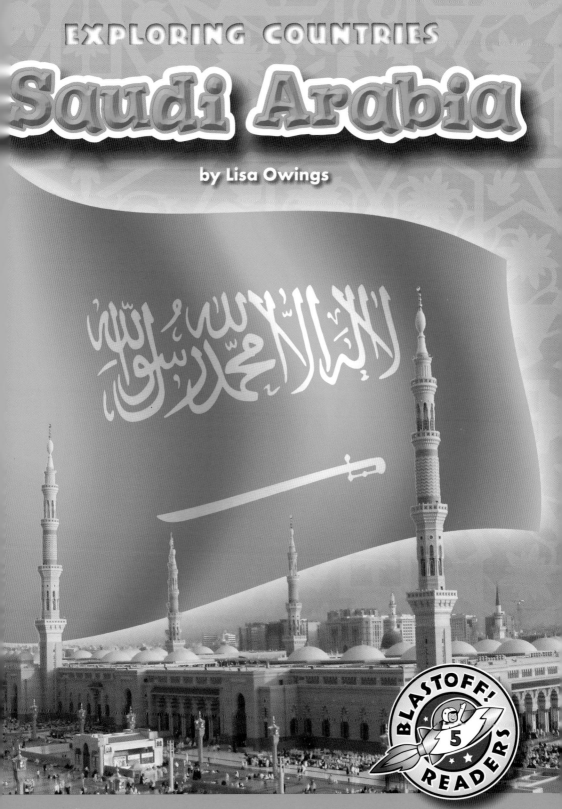

EXPLORING COUNTRIES
Saudi Arabia

by Lisa Owings

BLASTOFF! 5 READERS

BELLWETHER MEDIA • MINNEAPOLIS, MN

Note to Librarians, Teachers, and Parents:

Blastoff! Readers are carefully developed by literacy experts and combine standards-based content with developmentally appropriate text.

Level 1 provides the most support through repetition of high-frequency words, light text, predictable sentence patterns, and strong visual support.

Level 2 offers early readers a bit more challenge through varied simple sentences, increased text load, and less repetition of high-frequency words.

Level 3 advances early-fluent readers toward fluency through increased text and concept load, less reliance on visuals, longer sentences, and more literary language.

Level 4 builds reading stamina by providing more text per page, increased use of punctuation, greater variation in sentence patterns, and increasingly challenging vocabulary.

Level 5 encourages children to move from "learning to read" to "reading to learn" by providing even more text, varied writing styles, and less familiar topics.

Whichever book is right for your reader, Blastoff! Readers are the perfect books to build confidence and encourage a love of reading that will last a lifetime!

This edition first published in 2013 by Bellwether Media, Inc.

No part of this publication may be reproduced in whole or in part without written permission of the publisher. For information regarding permission, write to Bellwether Media, Inc., Attention: Permissions Department, 5357 Penn Avenue South, Minneapolis, MN 55419.

Library of Congress Cataloging-in-Publication Data
Owings, Lisa.
 Saudi Arabia / by Lisa Owings.
    p. cm. – (Blastoff! readers: exploring countries)
Includes bibliographical references and index.
Summary: "Developed by literacy experts for students in grades three through seven, this book introduces young readers to the geography and culture of Saudi Arabia"–Provided by publisher.
ISBN 978-1-60014-764-7 (hardcover : alk. paper)
 1. Saudi Arabia–Juvenile literature. I. Title.
DS204.25.O95 2013
953.8–dc23
                                        2012007664

Text copyright © 2013 by Bellwether Media, Inc. BLASTOFF! READERS and associated logos are trademarks and/or registered trademarks of Bellwether Media, Inc. SCHOLASTIC, CHILDREN'S PRESS, and associated logos are trademarks and/or registered trademarks of Scholastic Inc.

Printed in the United States of America, North Mankato, MN.

Contents

Where Is Saudi Arabia? 4

The Land 6

The Empty Quarter 8

Wildlife 10

The People 12

Daily Life 14

Going to School 16

Working 18

Playing 20

Food 22

Holidays 24

Mecca and the Hajj 26

Fast Facts 28

Glossary 30

To Learn More 31

Index 32

Jordan

Iraq

Kuwait

Qatar

Saudi Arabia

Riyadh ★

Red
Sea

Yemen

Arabian
Sea

4

Persian Gulf

UAE

Oman

N
W   E
S

Saudi Arabia is a country in the **Middle East**. It covers 830,000 square miles (2,149,690 square kilometers) of the Arabian **Peninsula**. The Red Sea separates Saudi Arabia from Africa to the west. The Persian **Gulf** laps against the country's eastern shores.

Jordan, Iraq, and Kuwait are Saudi Arabia's neighbors to the north. Qatar and the United Arab Emirates (UAE) lie to the east along the Persian Gulf. Yemen and Oman sit between the country's southern border and the Arabian Sea. Riyadh is the capital of Saudi Arabia. It stands near the center of the country.

Did you know?
Ancient volcanoes break up the landscape of western Saudi Arabia. Different minerals make some volcanoes black and others white.

Deserts spread across most of Saudi Arabia. The sands of the Rub' al-Khali cover the southern part of the country. In the north, wind whips An-Nafud into tall **dunes**. Ad-Dahna' connects these two deserts. The rocky Najd **plateau** rises in the center of the country. It slopes into the mountains that stretch along the Red Sea coast. In the east, **salt flats** and marshes dip to meet the Persian Gulf.

Red Sea

Najd plateau

Saudi Arabia has no permanent rivers or lakes. Water flows through valleys called *wadis* after it rains. Most of the country is hot and dry. Summer temperatures often rise above 110 degrees Fahrenheit (43 degrees Celsius).

Rub' al-Khali means "Empty Quarter" in Arabic. This desert covers more than one quarter of Saudi Arabia. It is the largest area of sand on Earth. Its sands also spill into Yemen, Oman, and the UAE. Only a few Bedouin tribes and brave explorers attempt to cross this vast desert.

Burnt orange dunes and pale valleys are carved by wind in the Rub' al-Khali. Sandstorms carry clouds of dust over the Empty Quarter and nearby cities. Daytime temperatures can reach more than 130 degrees Fahrenheit (54 degrees Celsius). Rain hardly ever falls to provide relief. At night, temperatures can drop below freezing. The **Milky Way** shines brightly overhead.

Rub' al-Khali

Did you know?

The world's largest oil field lies beneath the sands of the Empty Quarter. Its discovery in 1948 made Saudi Arabia the world's leading oil producer.

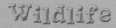

**Arabian
oryx**

The mountains and deserts of Saudi Arabia support a
variety of animals. Baboons and mountain goats scale
cliffs in the rocky west. Hunters once chased the Arabian
oryx across the country's deserts. Today, the oryx is
protected. Arabian wolves and sand cats slink across
the dunes in search of prey.

egret

honey badger

falcon

fun fact
Falcons in Saudi Arabia are often caught in the wild and trained to help people hunt. Hoods cover their eyes to keep them calm during training.

Mongooses and honey badgers pick fights with cobras. Lizards of all sizes scoot across the sand. Jerboas hop away from owls, eagles, and hawks. Flamingos and egrets wade along the coasts. The country's seas and **coral reefs** burst with fish and other sea creatures.

fun fact

Many native Arabs did not have permanent homes. They traveled with their herds of camels, goats, or sheep. The Bedouin peoples of Saudi Arabia still follow this lifestyle.

More than 26 million people call Saudi Arabia home. About nine out of every ten Saudis are Arabs. Their **ancestors** were **native** to the Arabian Peninsula. Other Saudis have ancestors from Africa or Asia. Many of them were religious **pilgrims**.

All Saudi **citizens** are Muslim. However, more than 5.5 million people living in Saudi Arabia are not citizens. They came from other countries to work in Saudi cities. These people are allowed to practice their own religions at home. Arabic is the official language of Saudi Arabia. Some businesspeople also speak English.

Speak Arabic!

Saudi Arabians use Arabic script when they write. However, Arabic words can be written in English to help you read them out loud.

English	Arabic	How to say it
hello	marhaba	MAR-hah-bah
good-bye	ma'as salaama	MA-as sa-LAM-ah
yes	na'am	nahm
no	la	lah
please	min fadlak	min FAD-lahk
thank you	shukran	SHOO-kran
friend (male)	sadiq	sah-DEEK
friend (female)	sadiqa	sah-DEEK-ah

Did you know?
Saudi men traditionally wear long white robes and head coverings. Women wear black *abayat* and veils to cover their bodies, heads, and faces.

Most Saudis live in modern cities such as Riyadh. However, their lives still focus on religion and **tradition**. All Saudis pray five times a day facing the holy city of Mecca. Many also wear traditional clothing. People travel by car, bus, or taxi. Women are not allowed to drive. Men must accompany them to large malls or outdoor markets called *souks*.

In the countryside, most people live with their relatives. Bedouin tribes wander with their herds and live in tents. Saudi farmers live in homes made of stone or mud. Most homes have separate rooms for women and men. It is considered improper for Saudi men and women to interact outside the home unless they are family.

Where People Live in Saudi Arabia

countryside 18%

cities 82%

Saudi boys and girls go to kindergarten together between ages 3 and 5. After that, they go to separate schools. Elementary school lasts for six years. Children study Arabic, art, history, math, and science. Islamic studies are a major part of education in Saudi Arabia.

Three years of middle school follow elementary school. Saudi students often begin learning English at this level. Most girls take **home economics**. Boys have physical education classes. High school students can choose to focus on Islamic studies. They can also pursue training for specific jobs. Many Saudis continue their education at universities in Saudi Arabia or **abroad**.

Did you know?
The King Abdullah University of Science and Technology was the first to allow women and men to attend classes together. It was founded in 2009.

17

Did you know?

Every Saudi citizen must pay the *zakat*. This tax is used to help feed, shelter, and clothe the poor.

Where People Work in Saudi Arabia

manufacturing 21%

farming 7%

services 72%

fun fact

Saudi women have more employment opportunities today than they did in the past. Still, fewer than one out of every five workers is female.

Saudi Arabia is a wealthy country. Large amounts of oil lie beneath its sands and seas. In cities, people work to turn this oil into fuel that is shipped all over the world. Factory workers also make chemicals, metals, and plastics. Saudi men work in shops and office buildings. Many women work in schools and hospitals.

In the countryside, farmers raise sheep, goats, and cattle for meat and milk. Chickens provide both meat and eggs. Only a small amount of land has enough water to grow food. Wheat and other grains are important crops. Farmers also grow tomatoes, melons, and dates.

! fun fact

In 2010, Saudi fashion designer Rania Khogeer helped Saudi women cheer on their favorite soccer teams. She created a sports-themed *abaya* for each team playing in the World Cup.

Saudis spend much of their free time with family and friends. Women visit with one another inside the home. Men play cards or attend sporting events. Young Saudis enjoy video games and chatting with friends on the Internet. Saudi Arabia has no movie theaters, but families like to watch movies at home.

Saudi boys and men are most active in sports. However, many schools now let Saudi girls play sports. The national passion is soccer. Camel races draw crowds of men to Riyadh. Saudis near the coasts swim, scuba dive, or windsurf in the country's warm seas.

Did you know?

During Ramadan, Saudis often enjoy pastries called *qatayef*. The pastries are filled with cheese, nuts, or spices. Saudis eat them in the evening after fasting all day!

qatayef

Saudis traditionally sit on the floor to eat their meals. They take food from a large platter. Main dishes are usually spicy. They often feature lamb or chicken with a side of rice. *Khuzi* is a favorite Bedouin dish of stuffed lamb. Families along the coasts enjoy shrimp and fish. Dates are a sweet dessert.

Seasoned meat called *shawarmah* can be wrapped in flatbread for lunch on the go. *Sambosas* are fried snacks that are especially popular during **Ramadan**. They are stuffed with mixtures of meat, vegetables, cheese, and spices. Coffee and tea are served throughout the day.

sambosas

khuzi

Ramadan

Saudis celebrate two official Muslim holidays each year. *Eid al-Fitr* marks the end of the holy month of Ramadan. Saudi families come together for three days of prayer and feasts. At dawn on the first day, they gather at **mosques** to offer a prayer of thanksgiving. Many buy new clothes for the occasion.

Eid al-Adha comes at the end of the traditional Muslim **pilgrimage** to Mecca. Many families sacrifice sheep or other animals. They prepare feasts using some of the meat. They give the rest of the meat to the poor.

> **! fun fact**
> National Day is quietly observed on September 23. Many Saudis spend the day shopping with family. People proudly wave their nation's flag in the streets.

National Day

Mecca

Only Muslims are allowed to enter the holy city of Mecca in Saudi Arabia. The **Prophet Muhammad** was born there. He founded the religion of Islam. According to Muhammad, all Muslims must try to make the *hajj* pilgrimage to Mecca at least once in their lives. During the *hajj*, men dress in two white cloths. Most women also wear white. Pilgrims first walk around the Kaaba **shrine** seven times. Then they touch or kiss the sacred Black Stone in the Kaaba.

Kaaba

Did you know?

Around 2 million Muslims make the *hajj* to Mecca each year.

! fun fact

All Muslims throughout the world face the Kaaba shrine at Mecca when they pray.

Over the next few days, pilgrims pray, perform **rituals**, and travel to holy places. Then they return to Mecca. This religious center brings Muslims together from across the globe. The *hajj* is a yearly reminder of Saudis' faith and commitment to tradition.

Saudi Arabia's Flag

The flag of Saudi Arabia features white Arabic script and a white sword on a green background. The script says, "There is no god but Allah, and Muhammad is the messenger of Allah." The color green represents Islam. This flag was officially adopted in 1973.

Official Name: Kingdom of Saudi Arabia

Area: 830,000 square miles (2,149,690 square kilometers); Saudi Arabia is the 13th largest country in the world.

Capital City:	Riyadh
Important Cities:	Jeddah, Mecca, Medina, Al-Dammam
Population:	26,534,504 (July 2012)
Official Language:	Arabic
National Holiday:	National Day (September 23)
Religion:	Muslim (100%)
Major Industries:	fuel, manufacturing, services, farming, construction
Natural Resources:	oil, natural gas, iron ore, gold, copper
Manufactured Products:	fuel, chemicals, metals, plastics, cement, fertilizer
Farm Products:	sheep, chickens, eggs, milk, wheat, barley, tomatoes, melons, dates
Unit of Money:	Saudi riyal; the riyal is divided into 100 halalas.

Glossary

abroad—outside of one's home country

ancestors—relatives who lived long ago

citizens—members of a nation; people have certain rights and responsibilities as citizens.

coral reefs—underwater structures made of coral; reefs usually grow in shallow seawater.

dunes—hills of sand formed by wind or water

gulf—part of an ocean or sea that extends into land

home economics—the study and practice of managing a home; cooking, cleaning, and childcare are some topics of home economics.

Middle East—a region of the world made up of northeastern Africa and southwestern Asia

Milky Way—the galaxy to which our solar system belongs; the Milky Way is made up of billions of stars.

mosques—buildings that Muslims use for worship

native—originally from a specific place

peninsula—a section of land that extends out from a larger piece of land and is almost completely surrounded by water

pilgrimage—a trip to a holy place

pilgrims—people who travel to a holy place to worship

plateau—an area of flat, raised land

Prophet Muhammad—the founder of Islam; Muslims believe Muhammad was a prophet and messenger of God, or Allah.

Ramadan—the ninth month of the Islamic calendar; Ramadan is a time when Muslims do not eat between sunrise and sunset.

rituals—acts that are always performed in the same way, often as part of a religious ceremony

salt flats—flat areas where saltwater has dried up, leaving the salt behind

shrine—a place, building, or object that is considered holy

tradition—a custom, idea, or belief handed down from one generation to the next

To Learn More

AT THE LIBRARY

McCaughrean, Geraldine. *One Thousand and One Arabian Nights*. New York, N.Y.: Oxford University Press, 1999.

Senker, Cath. *Saudi Arabia*. North Mankato, Minn.: Smart Apple Media, 2008.

Tracy, Kathleen. *We Visit Saudi Arabia*. Hockessin, Del.: Mitchell Lane Publishers, 2011.

ON THE WEB

Learning more about Saudi Arabia is as easy as 1, 2, 3.

1. Go to www.factsurfer.com.

2. Enter "Saudi Arabia" into the search box.

3. Click the "Surf" button and you will see a list of related Web sites.

With factsurfer.com, finding more information is just a click away.

Index

activities, 20, 21
Arabian Peninsula, 5, 12
capital (see Riyadh)
climate, 7, 8
clothing, 14, 20, 24, 26
daily life, 14-15
deserts, 6, 8, 9, 10
education, 16-17
Eid al-Adha, 25
Eid al-Fitr, 24
Empty Quarter, 8-9
food, 22-23
Hajj, 26, 27
holidays, 24-25
housing, 15
Kaaba, 26, 27
landscape, 6-9
languages, 13, 16
location, 4-5
Mecca, 14, 25, 26, 27
Najd plateau, 6, 7
National Day, 25
people, 8, 12, 13
Ramadan, 22, 23, 24
religions, 13, 14, 24, 25, 26, 27
Riyadh, 4, 5, 14, 21
sports, 20, 21

transportation, 14
wildlife, 10-11
working, 18-19